J 220.9

Sim

God is With Us

Simon, Mary Manz

DATE DUE

JAN 0 6 2002	
JUN 2 3 2002	
DEC 1 5 2002	
OCT 2 8 2007	
NOV 2 5 2007	
OCT 2 4 2010	

Name

Date

Presented by

First Inspirational Press edition published in 1998.

Inspirational Press
A division of BBS Publishing Corporation
386 Park Avenue South
New York, NY 10016

Inspirational Press is a registered trademark of BBS Publishing Corporation.

Published by arrangement with Concordia Publishing House,
3558 S. Jefferson Ave., St. Louis, MO 63118-3968.

Library of Congress Catalog Card Number: 97-77418
ISBN: 0-88486-205-4

Printed in Mexico.

God Is With Us

Beginning Bible Stories by

MARY MANZ SIMON

ILLUSTRATED BY DENNIS JONES

Hide the Baby
(The Birth of Moses)

Toot! Toot!
(The Fall of Jericho)

Bing!
(David and Goliath)

Whoops!
(Jonah and the Fish)

A HEAR ME READ GIFT COLLECTION

*An Inspirational Press Book
for Children*

To the Adult:

Early readers need two kinds of reading. They need to be read to, and they need to do their own reading. The Hear Me Read Bible Stories series helps you to encourage your child with both kinds.

For example, your child might read this book as you sit together. Listen attentively. Assist gently, if needed. Encourage, be patient, and be very positive about your child's efforts.

Then perhaps you'd like to share the selected Bible story in an easy-to-understand translation or paraphrase.

Using both types of reading gives your child a chance to develop new skills and pride in reading. You share and support your child's excitement.

As a mother and a teacher, I anticipate the joy your child will feel in saying, "Hear me read Bible stories!"

Mary Manz Simon

Hide the Baby

Exodus 2:1–10

(The Birth of Moses)

To Jeanette May
mentor and friend
Proverbs 19:20–21

Oh, a baby.

Hush, baby, hush.

Sleep, baby, sleep.

God will take care of you.

Oh, soldiers are coming.

The soldiers are coming!

Hide the baby.

Hush, baby, hush.

Sleep, baby, sleep.

God will take care of you.

Oh, soldiers are coming.

The soldiers are coming!

Hide the baby.

Hush, baby, hush.

Sleep, baby, sleep.

God will take care of you.

Oh, a baby.

Hush, baby, hush.

Hush, baby, hush.

Will you take care of the baby?

Hush, baby, hush.

Sleep, baby, sleep.

God will take care of you.

Toot! Toot!

Joshua 5:13–6:20
(The Fall of Jericho)

For Angela Michelle Simon
1 John 4:7–8

Jericho was big.

Jericho had big walls.

Jericho had big gates.

Jericho was big.

Joshua said to God,

"How can the people get in?

Jericho has big walls.

Jericho has big gates."

God said to Joshua,

"The people can get in."

"March around Jericho.

March around the big walls.

March around the big gates.

Toot the trumpets," said God.

March 2–3–4.

March 2–3–4.

Toot!

Toot!

"How can the people get in?"

Joshua said to God.

God said to Joshua,

"March around Jericho again.

March around the big walls again.

March around the big gates again.

Toot the trumpets again."

March 2–3–4.

March 2–3–4.

Toot!

Toot!

"Again," said God.

"March and toot.

March and toot."

"Again," said God.

"Again," said God.

March 2–3–4.

March 2–3–4.

Toot! Toot!

The walls fell.

The gates fell.

Jericho fell.

Toot!

Toot!

Praise God!

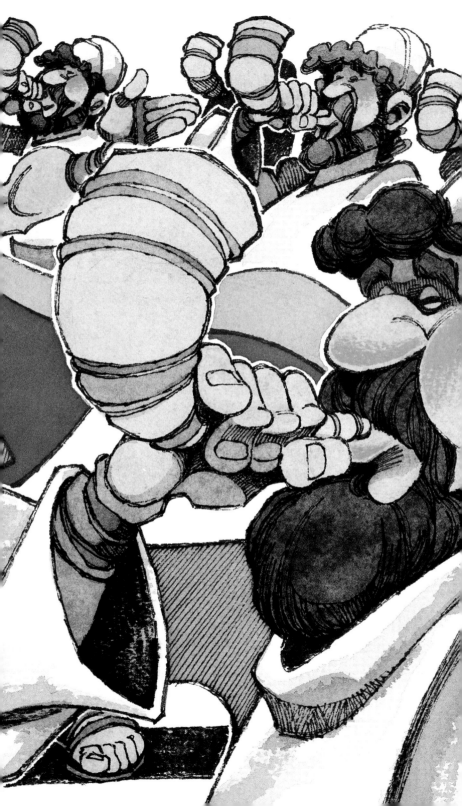

Bing!

1 Samuel 17:1–52
(David and Goliath)

For Matthew Michael Simon
1 John 3:1

Goliath was a big soldier.

Goliath had armor.

Goliath had a helmet.

Goliath had a sword.

Goliath teased the soldiers.

"Who will fight me?"

Goliath teased.

The soldiers looked at Goliath.

The soldiers looked at the armor.

"Who will fight me?"

Goliath teased.

The soldiers looked at the helmet.

The soldiers looked at the sword.

"No," said the soldiers.

"Who will fight Goliath?"

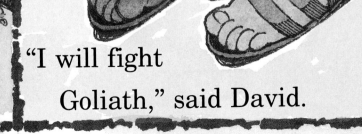

"I will fight
Goliath," said David.

The soldiers looked at David.

David was little.

The soldiers looked at Goliath.

Goliath was big.

Goliath had armor.

Goliath had a helmet.

Goliath had a sword.

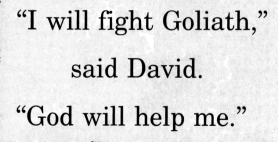

"I will fight Goliath,"
said David.
"God will help me."

"I will help," said the soldier.

The soldier had armor.

The soldier had a helmet.

The soldier had a sword.

"No," said David.

"God will help me.

God will help me fight Goliath."

Goliath looked at little David.

David looked at big Goliath.

David looked at the armor.

David looked at the helmet.

David looked at the sword.

"God helped me," said David.

"God helped me fight Goliath."

Whoops!

Jonah 1, 2, 3:1–3
(Jonah and the Fish)

For Matthew
Luke 18:16

"Go," said God.

"Go to the city.

Go to the city now."

"Tell the people about Me," said God.

"Tell the people I am God."

'I do not want to go," said Jonah.

'I do not want to go to the city.”

"I will not go to the city," said Jonah.

"I will not go to the city now."

"I will go away from God,"

said Jonah.

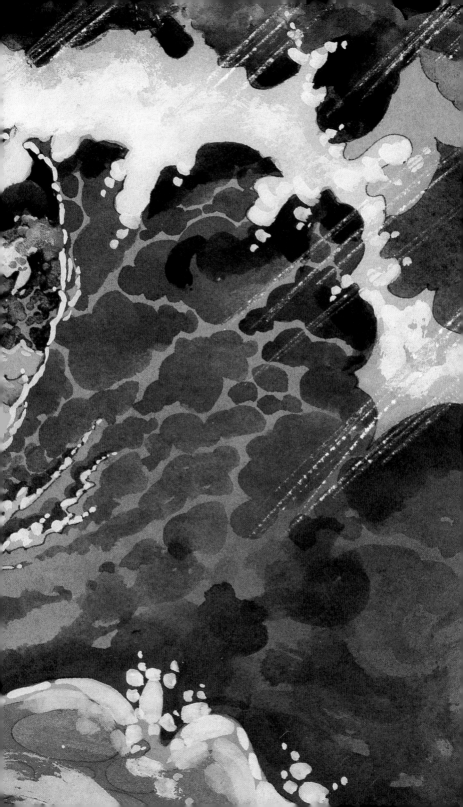

Whoops!

"I did not want to go to the city,"
said Jonah.
"I wanted to go away from God."

"Now I am sorry," said Jonah.

"I am sorry I wanted to

go away from God.

I am sorry I did not

go to the city."

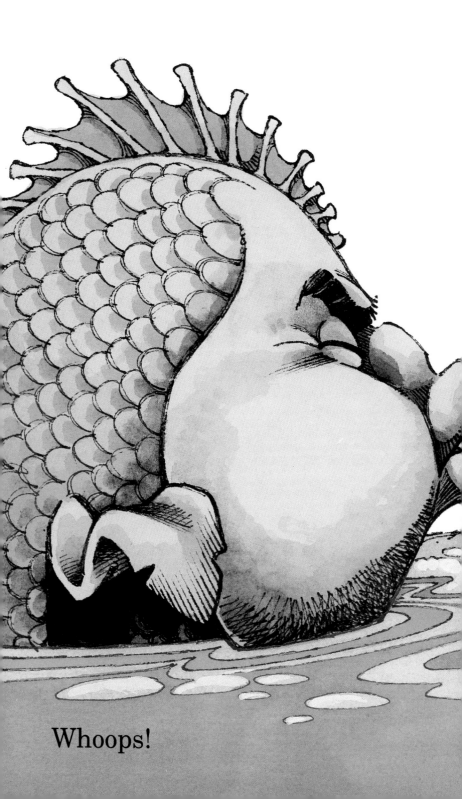

Whoops!

"Go," said God.

"Go to the city.

Go to the city now."

"Tell the people about Me," God said.
"Tell the people I am God."

"I will go," said Jonah.
"I will go now."

"I will go to the city," said Jonah.
"I will tell the people
about God."

Dr. Mary Manz Simon holds a doctorate in education with a specialty in early childhood education. She has taught students at every level from preschool to graduate school. She is a contributing editor for *Christian Retailing* and *Christian American*, a member of the Editorial board for *Christian Parenting Today*, and a columnist for *Virtue* and *Parent Life* magazines. Mary is a popular media personality, who has appeared on as many as 150 radio and television shows annually. Since her first book, *Little Visits with Jesus*, was released in 1987, her thirty-seven titles have sold more than one million copies and are published in seven languages. She lives in Belleville, Illinois.